The Centenary Collection

GETTING AROUND

TRAVEL IN OLD AUSTRALIA

The Five Mile Press

Getting Around

Travel in Old Australia

There wouldn't be a modern Australia without the story of transport in old Australia: getting to, and getting around. The country was settled by convicts and officials, both groups sentenced to transportation to New South Wales for differing periods of time and with different prospects. Without the notion of 'transportation', and the means to carry it out, Australia would have developed in quite different ways.

Aboriginal Australians had for tens of thousands of years their own ways of getting around the country, with little disturbance of the natural ebbs and flows. The European sensibility was quite different. Moving around and finding out about the country was a priority from the beginning. Early exploration by sea expanded the limits of settlement, as did crossing the Blue Mountains west of Sydney. Exploration continued by boat, by horse and by camel, until all the extremities had been reached.

On the land, horsepower was always important, whether in the form of horse-drawn transport to the railheads and river ports, hauling wool bales, or getting into town to buy supplies. Bullocks and bullockies had a strong impact where the roads were no better than tracks. The riverboats also became a vital inland transport system.

The gold boom meant that the Australian colonies, especially Victoria and New South Wales, developed a transport infrastructure, especially railways and ports in that great age of invention and innovation, the Victorian Age. New technology such as steam, and later electricity, and the internal combustion engine, had an important impact on transport in the cities of Australia, and travelling between them as well. The horse remained vital, both for personal transport and cartage, but it was rail – carrying cable and electric trams, and steam trains – that became dominant.

The sea had always been Australia's connection to the outside world, but a faster way was invented and Australians took to flying with great enthusiasm.

The internal combustion engine began to power pioneer cars on some surprisingly long journeys in the early years of the century, and Australia's greatest love affair with any form of transport took hold. Australia's long distances and terrain was made for the motor car. Getting around had never been easier.

Bullock Team in Julia Street, Portland, 1880s

Bullock teams were the road trains of old Australia, able to pull prodigious loads and capable of dealing with most of the problems of the rough bush tracks, from bogs to washaways. They pulled wagons laden with timber, piled high with wool bales, filled with the freight of general commerce. The bullockies lived their lives on the road, often with their families trailing behind, and had a reputation for hard drinking, foul language and cruelty to their animals. The reality was often different, as some men set themselves on the path to success from the freight rate of £4 per ton per 100 miles (160 kilometres). Sidney Kidman, the richest man in Australia in his time, started out with a bullock team. The old sweat and his tired dog in the Victorian town of Portland look to have seen many miles of hard road.

E.W.
ROW BR
WATCHMAKERS & JEWELLERS

Double-decker Horse Trams, South Australia, 1909

In 1906 the Adelaide Municipal Tramways Trust was given the job of electrifying the Adelaide tramway network, and it soon acquired all the horse tram companies within ten kilometres of the city. The first wires were erected on 21 May 1908, and the first electric trams commenced service on 9 March 1909. The last of Adelaide's beloved double-decker horse trams, such as the pair in the picture, was pulled by a sturdy pair from Goodwood to Clarence Park on 25 June 1914. Electrification was perhaps inevitable, but the end of the horse tram years also spelled an end to Adelaide as a big, charming country town.

104
GOOD

Spit Tram Transported by Barge

Sydney's first tram was a horse-drawn car that ran along Pitt Street from the (first) Redfern Station (between present-day Central and Redfern stations) to Circular Quay in 1861. It was an ill-engineered track, with an unstable bed, and rails that ran above the surface of the road. The death of prominent musician Isaac Nathan, crushed by a tram in 1864, caused public outcry and a parliamentary inquiry, resulting in the closure of the service in 1866. Steam trams were next in 1879, a technological marvel brought in for the Sydney International Exhibition. As well, a cable car service operated on the steep gradient of North Sydney, from Milson's Point in 1886. Sydney's geography dictated that tramlines didn't always connect with each other, resulting in many innovations. Here at the Spit, Middle Harbour, a punt carries a tram across the water.

Redfern Station, Steam Tram and Trains

Sydney's tram network expanded rapidly in the 19th century – such that it carried 93 million passengers in 1901. But until the late 1890s it was essentially a government-run steam tram system, with two cable systems supplementing it. Electrification had been first mooted in 1888, but the first electric system along New South Head Road, did not open until 1898, and the main George Street electric line did not open until 1899. A steam tram can be seen in the photograph at the old Redfern interchange, with a line-up of cabs, and trains in the background.

RAILWAY STATION, SYDNEY.
SYDNEY

Lady Boards Electric Tram, Brisbane, 1910s

A lady is determined to board the tram while the driver, in the fashion of tram drivers everywhere, is oblivious to her needs. This Brisbane electric tramcar was known as a 'combination car' – because it combined the enclosed compartment with a smokers' section at the back, for men, and the ladies', children's and old men's compartment at the front. Trams came to Brisbane in 1885 – and were horse-drawn. The tramway system was not genuinely popular until its takeover by the Brisbane Tramways Co. in 1895. Their success was partly due to the contract, which allowed the company to sell electricity to households along the routes they were electrifying. Electricity arrived in 1897, and rapidly replaced the old horse trams.

NEW FARM.W'GABBA.BOGGO Rd Jn
30
BRISBANE

Laying Tramlines in Perth

Trams came late to Perth. The city by-passed the horse and cable car stage, and went straight into electric trams, after a few years of missed opportunities, in 1899. In this picture of the construction of track for the Perth Electric Tramways Limited, it seems every boy, his sister and dog have come down for a look. The company was so keen it began construction a month before it had permission. Perth people were so enthusiastic about the whole business that, when word got out that there was to be a 'secret' late Sunday night trial run, it was met with a massive crowd.

UNDERTAKE
EMBALME
UNDERTAKER & GENERAL FUNERAL FURNISHER.
EMBALM

Barrack Street, Perth, 1901

One notable feature of Perth trams in the early days was the wire-mesh contraption to be seen on the back of this tram travelling down Barrack Street. At the front of the tram the mesh was lowered on a chain to project in front of the tram, rather like a cow-catcher on a train. In Perth these devices were called 'people-catchers' and as far as is known, were unique to West Australian trams. Trams ran in Perth until 1958. One notable driver was Albert Facey, famous for his autobiography *A Fortunate Life*.

OKMAN
W.G. BROOKMAN
WELLINGTON ST
J. VERRIER.
BOOT-MAKER.
REPAIRS A SPECIALITY
VOTE FOR W.G BROOKMAN
ESPLANADE
OP

First Electric Tram, Melbourne, 1889

This is the first electric tramcar to run in Australia. It was brought to Melbourne for the great Centennial Exhibition of 1888, where it proved a great success. However, there was no electric tram system in Melbourne to make use of the tramcar after the exhibition. The tram was eventually acquired by an enterprising property developer who installed it to run between suburban Box Hill rail station and the new development of Doncaster. It was an amateurish affair that ran from 1889 to 1896. Melbourne's first permanent electric tramway system did not open until 1906.

Cable Trams, Melbourne, 1905

Cable trams first operated in Melbourne from 1885, and the complete 70-kilometre system was in operation by 1891. Melburnians took to cable trams likes ducks to water – it was another civil engineering marvel in the days of 'Marvellous Melbourne', and was primarily the vision of a former American Francis B. Clapp. Cable trams operated by gripping onto the cable running beneath the streets, the cable travelling at a constant, smooth and silent 20 mph (32 kph). The front car was called, for mysterious reasons, the 'dummy' and was the place where the gripman operated the tram. Twenty people could be seated in the dummy, with additional 'hangers-on' standing on the footplate. The trailer was called 'the car' in Melbourne and could carry twenty-two seated passengers and thirty-four standing. Until the 1920s trams were painted in distinctive colours depending on their route. This St Kilda to North Carlton tram was green, with a white roof. The little roof on the dummy, in a pagoda shape, was known as the 'top-knot' and was lit with the appropriately coloured light to designate the route.

BRIGHTON ROAD
49
NORTH CARLTON & St KILDA.

Thomson's Steam Car, Melbourne, 1896

Herbert Thomson produced this 'steam phaeton' in the Melbourne suburb of Armadale in 1896, and to prove its reliability set out on an epic journey from Bathurst to Melbourne in April 1900 with mechanical engineer, Edward Holmes. The roads (and creeks) were not designed for such a contraption, which often had to be manhandled over the worst bits. Holmes complained, just a few hours out of Bathurst: 'We brought no eatables, so we felt awfully hungry and exhausted.' And they had nine days to go – the car covered the 800 kilometres at barely 14 kph. Only about ten of the kerosene-burning steam cars were made.

THOMSO
VIC.

First Motor Car Imported, 1897

John Pender a horseshoe-nail manufacturer of Brunswick, Victoria, saw a car like this at the Chicago Exhibition in 1896, and promptly ordered one from the inventor, Max Hertel. Powered by one gallon of stove naptha it travelled nine miles (14 kilometres) on its first journey in Australia, on 13 November, 1897. An ingenious one-lever operation involving a catch and ratchet made the crank shaft revolve, which filled the cylinders with the gas, and compressed it for ignition. Once the engine started the lever was released, holding back the catch. To stop the car the lever was pulled back to release the driving gears and apply the brakes to the wheels. The Hertel hurtled around Melbourne for five years, and is now in the Museum of Victoria.

Mrs Ben Thompson Reaches Gundagai

Mrs Ben Thompson of Adelaide, driving a single-cylinder six-horsepower Wolseley, was the only female competitor in Australia's first reliability trial – a five-day drive over rutted roads and tracks from Sydney to Melbourne in February 1905. 'The fact of a lady undertaking an arduous task like the present one over roads which are almost impassable in places has excited admiration and wonder,' wrote a newspaper of the day. Mrs Thompson, seen here being greeted in Gundagai, completed the course. Nine competitors finished without losing any points, and had to run a separate trial from Melbourne to Ballarat to determine the winner – which proved to be Colonel Tarrant in an Argyll. But the real winner was motoring itself, now demonstrably a competitive mode of transport in Australia.

Dunlop Reliability Trial

A second reliability trial, also sponsored by Dunlop, took place in November 1905, but this time it was from Melbourne to Sydney. So reliable were the motor cars that six completed the run without the loss of a single point. These cars were sent on a run to Medlow Bath, which again failed to separate five of the cars. The organisers then directed the quintet to drive back to Melbourne! They had completed 1276 miles (2054 kilometres) on paper-thin tyres over some of the roughest roads imaginable. Colonel Tarrant had built his own vehicle for the second trial, and was again in the winner's circle after the return trip. The picture shows the sort of roads confronted by the reliability trial drivers. It is captioned 'On the King's Highway: the main south coast road between Bodalla and Moruya, 1906.'

First Car from Adelaide to Darwin, 1908

This remarkable vehicle is a 25-horsepower Clement Talbot. It was the first car to complete the arduous and roadless 3400-kilometre journey from Adelaide to Darwin, in fifty-one days in 1908. And it was the second attempt by 29-year-old South Australian pioneer Henry Hamden Dutton and his mechanic Murray Aunger. The first, in a less powerful Talbot, had ground to a halt south of Tennant Creek the year before. They retrieved the first car, named *Angelina*, on the second trip in *The Overlander*. What is remarkable about *The Overlander* is that it went on to make the journey twice more – in 1958, driven by Henry Dutton's sons John and Geoffrey Dutton, and again in Australia's bicentennial year, 1988. The car, in tip-top condition, still runs, and is housed in the Birdwood Mill Museum in South Australia.

Scottish Rifles Test Motor Transport, 1910

A defence exercise in Sydney in 1910 envisaged an attack on Sydney Harbour by enemy battleships, engaging the attention of the big guns at the Heads. The 'enemy' silenced the guns at La Perouse, and landed a shore party with the intention of taking the South Head defenders from the rear. A message to the New South Wales defence force saw the Australian Volunteer Automobile Force crank into action. They quickly transported the Scottish Rifle Regiment to the scene, and defeated the invaders. The Automobile Force comprised thirty-nine motor cars, eleven commercial wagons and six motor cycles, valued at £33,000. The wagons could carry sixty-six soldiers, bristling with bayonets. The exercise once again demonstrated the efficacy and reliability of motor transport.

Scenic Drive, 1920s

It didn't take long for Australians to take motor cars to their hearts, and to take up the idea of just 'going for a drive' for the sheer pleasure of taking in the view. The car enabled Australia's predominantly city-dwelling population – the better-off among them anyway – to broaden their appreciation of Australia, and consequently put pressure on governments to build more roads. In Victoria the Great Ocean Road, with views like this, is evidence of this development. In 1921 there were 122,000 motor car drivers' licences in force, one licence for every 44.6 Australians. In 1933, with 761,000 licences in force, the proportion had risen to one licence for every 8.8 Australians.

Motor Mail, NSW, 1911

The first regular mail deliveries by motor were undertaken by John Cleary in 1911. Cleary is standing at right holding the seat of his Albion Motor Coach, travelling with passengers and post between Menindee, the telegraph relay station on the Darling River and Broken Hill. In a safeguard typical of new innovations in technology, the motor mail was only allowed to operate on the condition that the usual horse coach followed behind.

ALBION

Second Official Outing of (R)ACV, 1904

The (Royal) Automobile Club of Victoria staged its first run on 31 January 1904, when thirty motor cars and twenty motor cycles travelled 24 kilometres from Princes Bridge to the beach at Aspendale on Port Phillip Bay. The second outing, later in the year, was much further, some 90 kilometres to picturesque Marysville, in the foothills of the Great Divide. In winter it is snow country, hence the slightly alpine style of the buildings, but on a warm autumn afternoon the smartly yet casually dressed motorists look very comfortable. Scarved picture hats are *de rigeur* for the ladies, and dustcoats for the drivers. Of course, one chauffeur is wearing a uniform.

First Motor Built at Geelong, Victoria, 1906

'Progress' it says on the side of the first small motor omnibus produced in Geelong in 1906, and progress it was. Local motor body builders, after the introduction of the tariff on imported cars in 1902, began manufacturing bodies suited to local conditions, although often on imported chassis. The Ford Motor Company began its long association with vehicle manufacture in Geelong when the Canadian division opened a plant in 1925, to build bodies and assemble cars with imported chassis.

PROGRESS

Adelaide Motor Works, 1906

In 1902 a customs duty was levied on imported motor bodies in order to encourage local production. One company to take advantage of the burgeoning local industry was the Adelaide Motor Car Works, situated on the corner of Pulteney Street and Hindmarsh Square, pictured in 1906. By 1913 some 2000 bodies were being produced, and 5000 were imported. Higher tariffs in the 1920s saw local production soar to 90,000 in 1926–27, over one third of which were produced by Holden's Motor Body Builders in Adelaide – which produced its first body in 1917. In 1929 there were over half a million cars on Australia's roads.

THE ADELAIDE MOTOR WORKS & CARACE
THE ADELAIDE MOTOR CAR WORKS & GARAGE
THE ADELAIDE MOTOR CAR WORKS

Opening Hawkesbury River Bridge, 1889

By the late 1880s the New South Wales railway system had become two systems – one spreading from Sydney, and the other from Newcastle. In August 1887 the gap between the two systems was 20 kilometres – the line from Sydney had reached the bank of the Hawkesbury River, and that from Newcastle had made it to Gosford. The splendid stern-wheeled paddle-steamer *General Grant* ferried passengers and freight between the two railheads. In January 1888 the gap had been reduced to a mere 6 kilometres when the Newcastle line was extended to Millet Creek. The last major obstacle was the Hawkesbury River itself. An American firm, the Union Bridge Company, won the design and tender process, and built an 884-metre bridge in seven spans and piers. It was opened by the Governor of New South Wales Lord Carrington on 1 May 1889, and meant that travellers could make the great Australian railway journey from Brisbane to Adelaide, a distance of 2880 kilometres. They would have to make several changes of train, and endure three different gauges. The bridge was replaced in 1939.

OPENING DAY OF THE HAWKESBURY RIVER BRIDGE, N.S

Flinders Street Station, 1895

Flinders Street Station, once reputed to be the busiest suburban railway station in the world, was built in French Renaissance style in 1900, with a three-storey building running for a block, and a copper dome above the famous clocks on the corner of Swanston Street – Melbourne's most famous rendezvous. Back in 1895, Melbourne's suburban trains terminated in much less grand circumstances. The ramps take passengers up to Swanston Street and Princes Bridge, the trains carrying through to the east under the bridge.

WALLACH'S
CRAIG, WILLIAMSON
VICTORIAN BLACK COAL
UNION CHAMBERS
E.L.YENCKEN & Co
WINDOW GLASS
WALL PAPERS, OILS, COLOURS
ROCKE TOMPSITT
E.L.YENCKEN & Co
MARS & SAMSON
TEAS
COAL CREEK BUILDINGS

Opening Darwin to Pine Creek Railway, 1889

There was a wild gold-rush at Pine Creek, 250 kilometres south of Darwin in 1872, and soon a large town developed. Pine Creek had been named by the surveyors of the Overland Telegraph, in 1870, for the trees that looked like pines growing on the bank of the creek. Gold continued to be mined, especially by Chinese miners, permitted to come to the Northern Territory until 1888. A railway connecting the two major townships in Northern Australia seemed appropriate. The picture shows Judge Paper's wife baptising the locomotive *Port Darwin* before the opening of the line. Pine Creek remained as far south as you could go from Darwin by train until 1916, when the line was extended. But the great Darwin to Adelaide line was still on the drawing board.

PORT DARWIN

Last Glenelg Train, King William Street, Adelaide

In 1873 a private railway company opened a service from a station in King William Street, a major Adelaide street, to the beach-side suburb of Glenelg. The service was taken over by the South Australian Railways in 1899, and ran until 1914 on the South Australian gauge of 5 feet 3 inches (160 centimetres). After World War I, it was taken over by the Tramways Trust and converted to the standard tram gauge of 4 feet 8 inches (142 centimetres). The Glenelg line is the only one on which the maroon and cream trams still run in Adelaide.

HARRY LYONS
WALL PAPERS
EVERY EVENING
CAKES & PASTRY

Transporting Wool

Taking the old road, and the new. A Ford truck of the 1930s carts half the number of wool bales that the old-fashioned and painfully slow bullock wagon can manage. Bullock teams might have been slow, at just 5 to 10 miles a day, but in some areas of the bush, they could haul wool through muddy terrain that even modern vehicles could not penetrate. Bullocks became something of a specialisation even before motor competition, with horse teams taking over on easier routes where they could cover 12 to 18 miles a day.

5
L58-266

Bullocks Drawing Logs

Bullockies used the long stockwhip and a mastery of bad language to get their large teams to move. They had conditioned the animals to associate a violent curse with a painful crack of the whip, so that after a certain time they would move on at the first sound of cursing, the whip merely flicking the hide. The team in the picture is at least twenty beasts long and requires two bullockies to work it, dragging huge and heavy logs.

Cycling in Melbourne, 1895

In order to allay fears that cycling was unsuited to ladies, and might encourage evil in the hearts of men, cycle demonstrations or cycle church parades were organised. The bonneted ladies on their safety bicycles chat to their children, wearing what was coyly described as 'rational' dress, bloomers beneath their skirts. The men, on the same models, keep a weather eye out for errant horses and cabs. The man leading the pack is wearing an 'Athletic Shirt', where the collar can be removed while cycling, to be respectably replaced on reaching church or office.

Melbourne Penny-farthings, 1870s

Several technological breakthroughs in the 1870s spurred the development of the 'ordinary' or penny-farthing bicycle, which was an improvement on the unsatisfactory 'boneshaker' or velocipede. In this picture of a group of well-to-do enthusiasts the progress made can be seen. First, the big 152-centimetre front wheel meant that cyclists could pedal more slowly and still maintain stability. Tensioned wire spokes, applied to the bicycle in 1869, made the big wheels workable, and the use of hollow front forks with a small rear wheel lessened weight. Cushioned, hollow rubber tyres and a sprung seat made for a smoother ride. They were quite fast.

Tricycle, 1880s

In the 1880s quite a few cyclists felt more comfortable peddling a stable three wheels rather than a wobbly two. Many models were developed. The most popular one in America was the 'staunch and speedy' Victor Tricycle, of which the manufacturer, the Overman Wheel Co. of Chicopee, Massachusetts, boasted 'regarding this tricycle, if you should try one, I'll wager a new string of fancies you'll buy one'. It was a complicated machine with the small front wheel steering the tricycle by use of levers. Australian developments, such as the one in the picture, had the small wheel at the back, and steering directly with handlebars on the front. Tricycles were trialled by the post offices of the colonies in the 1880s, but proved unsatisfactory – especially in hilly Sydney.

Cycling Gold Digger

A studio portrait of a digger, who cycled from Coolgardie, Western Australia, to the rumoured gold-rush at Mt Ragged, east of Esperance in 1895, a 2500-kilometre round trip. Bush workers were great cyclists in the 1890s and beyond. Note the patched pneumatic tyres (invented in 1888) the saddlebag, the swag over his shoulder, the billy on the handlebar for water. He is a reminder of the famous cycling poem by 'Banjo' Paterson about another-bike loving miner – Mulga Bill:

'Twas Mulga Bill, from Eaglehawk, that caught the cycling craze;
He turned away his good old horse that served him many days;
He dressed himself in cycling clothes, resplendent to be seen;
He hurried off to town and bought a shining new machine;
And as he wheeled it through the door, with air of lordly pride,
The grinning shop assistant said, 'Excuse me, can you ride?'

RETURNED FROM Mt RAGGED RUSH
1000 MILES TRIP IN THE BUSH

Cycling Shearer

'The shearer set out on these trips exactly as if he were going from Sydney to Parramatta. He asked the way, lit his pipe, put his leg over his bicycle and shoved off,' wrote C.E.W. Bean, the great Australian historian of World War I. In his series of newspaper articles for the *Sydney Morning Herald*, as he travelled the backblocks in 1908, Bean was fascinated with the heavily laden bicyles of the bush. He realised that they travelled long distances more quickly than a horse, were cheaper to feed, and cheap to buy – prices of safety bicycles fell from £20 at the beginning of the decade to £6 or less at the end. They were disliked by horsemen, who saw them as a threat, somehow, to their way of life. But it wasn't the bike that was the threat. It was the motor.

A MODERN
AUSTRALIAN SHEARER.
2372. Kerry. Sydney.

Shipping at Darling Harbour, 1871

The port of Sydney had developed very haphazardly in the second half of the 19th century, and was not efficiently managed by the private interests which controlled most of the wharves from Circular Quay to Darling Harbour in the west, and around to Woolloomooloo Bay in the east. Darling Harbour is pictured in 1871, when the transport of goods and passengers was still very much the business of sail, and the unloading of cargo was a matter of horse and man power. A Marine Board of New South Wales was established in 1871 to oversee the administration of Australia's largest port. It ran the fiefdom for thirty years before a Royal Commission made an unfavourable report in 1897, and it was abolished. By this time the government had 'resumed' most wharves, and appointed the Sydney Harbour Trust to run them.

Loading Apples for England at Hobart

Captain Bligh of *Bounty* fame, planted the first apple tree in Tasmania (then Van Diemen's Land) in 1788 at Adventure Bay. By 1833 the *Van Diemen's Land Almanac* reported that the growth of apple growing 'was so astonishing that it needs to be seen to be credited'. Commercial cultivation took off in the 1840s, and the export income it provided to the colony was crucial to its survival and the expansion of ports such as Hobart. The port was a sorry state of affairs until the arrival of Governor Denison in 1847. He was responsible for the extension of the stone wharf at Battery Point, built in 1834, and the construction of Constitution Dock in 1849. In the picture, taken in the early 1900s at Constitution Dock, wagonloads of Tasmania's finest are being loaded for export to England.

Paddle-Steamer *Ruby*, 1908–09

The first Murray steamer was a model of bush ingenuity, the *Mary Ann*, built by William Randell at Noa-No near Mannum in South Australia. He and his brothers made a 55-foot (17-metre) red gum shallow draft hull, launching it in 1853. A local blacksmith made a boiler out of quarter-inch iron plate, which had the disconcerting habit of going out of shape under pressure. They acquired an old steam engine, and set sail on the mighty Murray. The *Mary Ann* began taking on cargo in March, and later that year made an epic voyage past Echuca to Moama, 1000 miles (1610 kilometres) from the sea. Soon many other steamers plied the river, carrying wool and live sheep, reducing transport time and cost considerably. The *Ruby* is pictured in the early years of the century. She was built for the river trade and touring.

RUBY

PS *Trafalgar* Towing Wool Barges on Murray

A contemporary description of the paddle-steamer the *Trafalgar* notes this boat was built in Echuca in 1878 on the model of Fulton's steamer plying the East River in New York. Her frames and ironwork were wrought by Forman's Foundry in Melbourne, and the engines manufactured by Robison Bros. The *Trafalgar* was 108 feet (33 metres) long, 18 feet six inches (5.5 metres) in beam, and had 7½ feet (2 metres) depth in her hold. 'She is the crack passenger boat on the Murray', the report says. Every river steamer has a satellite in the shape of a barge (seen in the photograph) towed by rope affixed to a short mast, called a 'hog-mast'. Some of these barges had a capacity of 250 tons (255 tonnes). 'It is afternoon when we go on board the *Trafalgar*. We are watched by NSW customs officers, but they make no objection to our extensive preparations for a drought. The cabin allotted to us is larger and more commodious than can be obtained on any ocean-going steamer, occupying the whole breadth of the house on the hurricane deck ... There is no bar on the *Trafalgar* or any of the river boats. All are run on temperance principles. Intending passengers should prepare for this emergency ...'

Lawrence Hargrave, 1894

Lawrence Hargrave was a pioneer aeronautical inventor, whose ideas in the design of wings, and engines had a lasting impact on early aviation. In this photograph Hargrave (left) is putting together four of his box kites above the beach at Stanwell Park in New South Wales in November 1894. They would lift him five metres off the ground, and he announced in the following year that 'A safe means of making an ascent with a flying machine...and descending, are now at the service of any experimenter.' This wing shape was the prototype of the early European aeroplanes. His previous work on a compressed air radial rotary engine, demonstrated in 1889, was also important: it was the ancestor of the engines that powered most of these early aeroplanes.

E
A
B
C
D

First Airmail in Australia, 1914

In June 1914 French airman Maurice Guillaux demonstrated the usefulness of the aeroplane in Australia by flying his Bleriot monoplane from Melbourne to Sydney in two-and-a-half days, 'descending here and there,' noted the *Sydney Morning Herald*, 'to renew his petrol in half the time that the train takes to cover the distance.' His flying time was just 9 hours and 15 minutes. The plane was carrying 1785 postcards weighing about 40 pounds (18 kilograms). Guillaux had meant to follow the railway line, but bad weather and fog meant he had to put down at various places, for directions in addition to petrol. He made it as far as Harden in New South Wales on the first day, and had to turn back and remain there on the second day because of the weather. On the third day he landed at Goulburn, and then set off for Moss Vale, where he was going to pick up a map – but the instead of landing among the trees on the golf course there he continued towards Sydney, without a map. He landed at Liverpool, obtained a map, and then proceeded to the Sydney Sports Ground. It was the first airmail flight in Australia, the first Melbourne–Sydney flight, and the longest airmail flight in the world.

First Flight from England to Australia, 1919

In 1919 Prime Minister Billy Hughes offered a prize of £10,000 for the first British aircraft manned by Australians to fly from London to Australia in 30 days. Captain Ross Smith and his brother Keith Smith, with Sergeants J.M. Bennett and W.H. Shiers as mechanics, began their epic journey on 12 November 1919 in a twin-engined Vickers Vimy. In 1918 Ross Smith had previously piloted a Handley Page bomber from Cairo to Calcutta, so he knew something of the conditions to be encountered. Bad weather over Europe and the Middle East, and a boggy airfield in Java, caused serious problems, but eventually the aircraft reached Darwin on 10 December – 28 days after leaving London. Flying time was 135 hours to cover 11,340 miles (18,260 kilometres). After further adventures and mechanical problems, the aircraft and crew completed a triumphal tour of Australia in Melbourne on 25 February 1920. The picture shows the crew boarding the Vimy at Mascot in Sydney on the last leg.

Qantas Expands Queensland Service, 1929

In 1919 former World War I flyers Hudson Fysh and P.J. McGinness landed the job of surveying the route and potential airfields for the London-Australia air racers, between Darwin and Queensland. They did this in a T-Model Ford, and reflected that there was great potential for aircraft to help in the development of outback Queensland. They met the third founder of what became Qantas (Queensland and Northern Territory Aerial Services) when they dragged grazier Fergus McMaster out of a bog in the Cloncurry River. The trio soon became enthusiastic about an outback air service, and registered the company at Winton in western Queensland on 16 November 1920 – capital £6037. Two war service aircraft – a BE 2E and an Avro 504K got the company airborne on air taxi and joy rides. By 1929 Qantas had acquired two powerful DH61's including the one in the picture, *Apollo*, which flew the first service into Brisbane from Charleville, on 23 April 1929. The service soon ran from Longreach, departing at 5.30 am Sundays, and reaching Brisbane at 3.30 pm, via Blackall, Tambo, Charleville, Roma and Toowoomba at a cost, for the whole trip, of under £15

QUEENSLAND AND NORTHERN TERRITO
AERIAL SERVICES LTD.
BRI
G.P.O.
AIR MAIL
QANTAS LTD
APOLLO

Scott and Black Win Air Race from Britain, 1934

To commemorate Victoria's Centenary, Sir McPherson Robertson, the philanthropist, confectioner and co-founder of MacRoberson Miller Aviation, donated a £10,000 prize for the fastest flight between London and Melbourne. It was won by C.W.A. Scott and T. Campbell Black, in the beautifully streamlined red-and-white DH 88 Comet, in a flying time of 70 hours, 54 minutes and 18 seconds. They took off from Mildenhall, England, at 6.34 am on 20 October and zoomed through the finish line at Flemington racecourse, Melbourne at 3.35 pm on 23 October – an elapsed time of two days, four hours and 33 minutes. This broke the old record by about four days. Even more astonishing was that the second and third places, filled by the new generation of commercial airliners, broke the old record too. A Douglas DC 2 flown by KLM came second, and an American entry, a Boeing 247D, third.

G-ACSS
G-A

Camel Team Halts outside Post Office

Australia's first camels arrived in Hobart in 1840. They were shipped to Melbourne in 1841, and then overlanded to Sydney, where a baby camel was born. They were bought for £225 by the New South Wales government and exhibited on the Sydney Domain. The first bulk stock was bought by the Victorian Government from India in 1860 for the Burke and Wills expedition. In 1865 Thomas Elder brought in 120 baggage camels for service in the interior, and in 1886 two Afghanis brought 259 of the beasts from India to carry cargo to the goldfields in Western Australia. Camels were used by explorers, to survey the Overland Telegraph and the Trans-Australia Railway and for all manner of pastoral, mining and fossicking transport. In the photograph, taken at the Black Flag post office and store – Black Flag is a now forgotten place somewhere in the wilds of Western Australia – a couple of prospectors rest and take the weight off their camels.

STORE
35 BLACK-FLAG STORE & POST OFFICE

Coachbuilder, 1885

The coachbuilder was the car dealer of his time, and new models and 'technological' breakthroughs were just as important as they are today. The master coachbuilder is sitting on the footpath, in front of nine assistants and apprentices and his wares. The two conveyances immediately beside the men are lightweight American-style buggies. When introduced to Australia in the 1860s it was immediately recognised that the two-person, four-wheel, one-horsepower design was ideally suited to Australian country tracks and rough urban roads. People could travel vast distances in much more comfort in buggies than on horseback, and they were ideal for trips from property to town for supplies. The two-wheel version, on the left, was called a jinker. Other larger and heavier wagons were also made and used on properties – the four-wheeled wagonette with facing seats along the sides and the four-wheeled phaeton with all seats facing the front. But these also required more horsepower.

F.W. JOHNSON
COACHBUILDER
COACH
BUILDE

Upper-class Family, 1880s

Guilty at being caught in a brand-new carriage outside a hotel, three generations of the bunyip aristocracy look down their noses at the camera, too polite to order the footman (just caught at left of the picture) to drive off. Grandmother looks particularly unhappy, perhaps reflecting on her less than upper-class background. Mother, at left, is wary, possibly sensing the photograph will eventually appear as a postcard. The daughters look daggers in our direction, while the two gentlemen at the rear, father and grandfather, are hostile. Perhaps the photographer wasn't dressed well enough for the possum-skin-covered ladies so lately raised to their new station in life.

ENTRANCE

Flinders Street Station at Elizabeth Street, 1870s

A couple of drivers wait with their two-horse wagonettes outside Flinders Street Station in the 1870s. They await passengers who will come over the viaduct on the St Kilda line, and will take them through the city and then down Rathdowne and Lygon streets to North Carlton, or down Elizabeth Street to Hotham, as North Melbourne was then known. The posts that can be seen at the left of the photograph raised the tower clock. There has been a clock facing up Elizabeth Street ever since. The original clock was replaced by the present one in 1905. The old clock was sent to Spencer Street, to face down Collins Street, where it remained until the 1960s.

LEWIS & WHITTY'S
ODORBANE
THE GREAT DEODORANT
ISINFECTANT.
RAILWAY
ROOMS
LUNCHEON
ROOMS
NORTH CARLTON, RATHDOWNE & LYGON
W.T. CLARK
RUBBER
STAMP

Horse Van Parcel Express

At the end of the 19th century, the equivalent to the courier services of today was the cut-throat business of the parcel express. These determined Western Australian chaps would meet the ships as they arrived in Fremantle from Britain and Europe, carrying the latest in newspapers and magazines, dress materials and fashion items, and try to be the first to get them into Perth – and Australia – after a 20 kilometre gallop. Behind them is a carriage works of a type once to be found in virtually every town in Australia.

PIONEER
CARRIAGE WORK
PAINTING
HUGH FALCON
CREWS & MOORHOUSE
CARRIAGE BU
PARCELS
EXPRESS
CUSTOMS
HOUSE
PERTH
Perth & Fremantle
PARCELS
EXPRESS
HOUSE
CARRIERS.

Leviathan Coach at Cobb & Co. Office, Geelong

Cobb & Co., the name synonymous with coaching in Australia, was founded by four Americans in 1853, including Freeman Cobb. They imported a number of leather-sprung American coaches and commenced services from Melbourne to Port Melbourne in 1854, and then to the goldfields. After making a large profit the partners sold out and the company was eventually reorganised by James Rutherford, with headquarters in Bathurst, in 1862. Competition with railways forced it to service the bush areas that rail couldn't reach, and it prospered for fifty years. The last run was in 1924. The coach in the photograph was the *Leviathan*, its twelve grey horses driven by 'Cabbage Tree' Ned Devine. Pictured in Geelong in 1862, the great coach was transporting the English cricket team around the country for each of its engagements. At the conclusion of the tour the much-loved driver was given a purse of 300 sovereigns.

COACH
COBB & Co
OFFICE.

The Five Mile Press Pty Ltd
22 Summit Road
Noble Park Victoria 3174
Australia

First published in 2000

Designer: Sonia Juraja

Printed in China

National Library of Australia Cataloguing-in-Publication data:
Old Australia: the centenary collection. Getting around: travel in old Australia

ISBN 1 86503 296 4.

1. Transportation - Australia - History - Pictorial works. 2. Transportation - Australia - Pictorial works. 3. Local transit - Australia - History - Pictorial works. 4. Local transit - Australia - Pictorial works. 5. Urban transportation - Australia - History - Pictorial works. 6. Urban transportation - Australia - Pictorial works. I. Title.

388.0994